1

This book belongs to:

_____

FAIRY MOON
2022

Fairy Moon 2022
Journal

Copyright © 2021 by Crystal Sky
www.psychic-emails.com

Mystic Cat

The information accessible from this book is for informational purposes only. No statement within is a promise of benefits. There is no guarantee of any results.

Images are under license from Shutterstock, Dreamstime, or Deposit-photos.

2022

JANUARY
M	T	W	T	F	S	S
					1	2
3	4	5	6	7	8	9
10	11	12	13	14	15	16
17	18	19	20	21	22	23
24	25	26	27	28	29	30
31						

FEBRUARY
M	T	W	T	F	S	S
	1	2	3	4	5	6
9	10	11	12	11	12	13
14	15	16	17	18	19	20
21	22	23	24	25	26	27
28						

MARCH
M	T	W	T	F	S	S
	1	2	3	4	4	6
7	8	9	10	11	12	13
14	15	16	17	18	19	20
21	22	23	24	25	26	27
28	29	30	31			

APRIL
M	T	W	T	F	S	S
				1	2	3
4	5	6	7	8	9	10
11	12	13	14	15	16	17
18	19	20	21	22	23	24
25	26	27	28	29	30	

MAY
M	T	W	T	F	S	S
						1
2	3	4	5	6	7	8
9	10	11	12	13	14	15
16	17	18	19	20	21	22
23	24	25	26	27	28	29
30	31					

JUNE
M	T	W	T	F	S	S
		1	2	3	4	5
6	7	8	9	10	11	12
13	14	15	16	17	18	19
20	21	22	23	24	25	26
27	28	29	30			

JULY
M	T	W	T	F	S	S
				1	2	3
4	5	6	7	8	9	10
11	12	13	14	15	16	17
18	19	20	21	22	23	24
25	26	27	28	29	30	31

AUGUST
M	T	W	T	F	S	S
1	2	3	4	5	6	7
8	9	10	11	12	13	14
15	16	17	18	19	20	21
22	23	24	25	26	27	28
29	30	31				

SEPTEMBER
M	T	W	T	F	S	S
			1	2	3	4
5	6	7	8	9	10	11
12	13	14	15	16	17	18
19	20	21	22	23	24	25
26	27	28	29	30		

OCTOBER
M	T	W	T	F	S	S
					1	2
3	4	5	6	7	8	9
10	11	12	13	14	15	16
17	18	19	20	21	22	23
24	25	26	27	28	29	30
31						

NOVEMBER
M	T	W	T	F	S	S
	1	2	3	4	5	6
7	8	9	10	11	12	13
14	15	16	17	18	19	20
21	22	23	24	25	26	27
28	29	30				

DECEMBER
M	T	W	T	F	S	S
			1	2	3	4
5	6	7	8	9	10	11
12	13	14	15	16	17	18
19	20	21	22	23	24	25
26	27	28	29	30	31	

2023

JANUARY
M	T	W	T	F	S	S
						1
2	3	4	5	6	7	8
9	10	11	12	13	14	15
16	17	18	19	20	21	22
23	24	25	26	27	28	29
30	31					

FEBRUARY
M	T	W	T	F	S	S
		1	2	3	4	5
6	7	8	9	10	11	12
13	14	15	16	17	18	19
20	21	22	23	24	25	26
27	28					

MARCH
M	T	W	T	F	S	S
		1	2	3	4	5
6	7	8	9	10	11	12
13	14	15	16	17	18	19
20	21	22	23	24	25	26
27	28	29	30	31		

APRIL
M	T	W	T	F	S	S
					1	2
3	4	5	6	7	8	9
10	11	12	13	14	15	16
17	18	19	20	21	22	23
24	25	26	27	28	29	30

MAY
M	T	W	T	F	S	S
1	2	3	4	5	6	7
8	9	10	11	12	13	14
15	16	17	18	19	20	21
22	23	24	25	26	27	28
29	30	31				

JUNE
M	T	W	T	F	S	S
			1	2	3	4
5	6	7	8	9	10	11
12	13	14	15	16	17	18
19	20	21	22	23	24	25
26	27	28	29	30		

JULY
M	T	W	T	F	S	S
					1	2
3	4	5	6	7	8	9
10	11	12	13	14	15	16
17	18	19	20	21	22	23
24	25	26	27	28	29	30
31						

AUGUST
M	T	W	T	F	S	S
	1	2	3	4	5	6
7	8	9	10	11	12	13
14	15	16	17	18	19	20
21	22	23	24	25	26	27
28	29	30	31			

SEPTEMBER
M	T	W	T	F	S	S
				1	2	3
4	5	6	7	8	9	10
11	12	13	14	15	16	17
18	19	20	21	22	23	24
25	26	27	28	29	30	

OCTOBER
M	T	W	T	F	S	S
						1
2	3	4	5	6	7	8
9	10	11	12	13	14	15
16	17	18	19	20	21	22
23	24	25	26	27	28	29
30	31					

NOVEMBER
M	T	W	T	F	S	S
		1	2	3	4	5
6	7	8	9	10	11	12
13	14	15	16	17	18	19
20	21	22	23	24	25	26
27	28	29	30			

DECEMBER
M	T	W	T	F	S	S
				1	2	3
4	5	6	7	8	9	10
11	12	13	14	15	16	17
18	19	20	21	22	23	24
25	26	27	28	29	30	31

2022 Full Moons

Wolf Moon: January 17th, 23:48.

Snow Moon: February 16th, 16:57

Worm Moon March 18th, 07:17

Pink Moon: April 16th, 18:54

Flower Moon: May 16th, 04:13

Strawberry Moon: June 14th, 11:51

Buck Moon: July 13th, 18:37

Sturgeon Moon: August 12th, 01:35

Corn, Harvest Moon: September 10th, 09:59

Hunters Moon: October 9th, 20:54

Beaver Moon: November 8th, 11:01

Cold Moon: December 8th, 04:07

2022 At A Glance

Eclipses

Partial Solar – April 30th

Total Lunar – May 16th

Partial Solar – October 25th

Total Lunar -November 8th

Equinoxes and Solstices

Spring - March 20th

Summer - June 21st

Fall – September 23rd

Winter – December 21st

Mercury Retrogrades

January 14th, Aquarius - February 4th Capricorn

May 10th, Gemini - June 3rd, Taurus

September 10th, Libra - October 2nd Virgo

December 29th, Capricorn - January 1st, 2023, Capricorn

The Moon Phases

- ⬤ New Moon (Dark Moon)
- ⬤ Waxing Crescent Moon
- ◑ First Quarter Moon
- ◯ Waxing Gibbous Moon
- ◯ Full Moon
- ◯ Waning Gibbous (Disseminating) Moon
- ◑ Third (Last/Reconciling) Quarter Moon
- ⬤ Waning Crescent (Balsamic) Moon

● New Moon (Dark Moon)

The New Moon reveals what hides beyond the realm of everyday circumstances. It creates space to focus on contemplation and the gathering of wisdom. It is the beginning of the moon cycles. It is a time for plotting your course and planning for the future. It does let you unearth new possibilities when you tap into the wisdom of what is flying under the radar. You can embrace positivity, change, and adaptability. Harness the New Moon's power to set the stage for developing your trailblazing ideas. It is a Moon phase for hatching plans for nurturing ideas. Creativity is quickening; thoughts are flexible and innovative. Epiphanies are prevalent during this time.

● Waxing Crescent Moon

It is the Moon's first step forward on her journey towards fullness. Change is in the air, it can feel challenging to see the path ahead, yet something is tempting you forward. Excitement and inspiration are in the air. It epitomizes a willingness to be open to change and grow your world. This Moon often brings surprises, good news, seed money, and secret information. This Moon brings opportunities that are a catalyst for change. It tempts the debut of wild ideas and goals. It catapults you towards growth and often brings a breakthrough that sweeps in and demands your attention. Changes in the air, inspiration weaves the threads of manifestation around your awareness.

◗ First Quarter Moon

The First Quarter Moon is when exactly half of the Moon is shining. It signifies that action is ready to be taken. You face a crossroads; decisive action clears the path. You cut through indecisiveness and make your way forward. There is a sense of something growing during this phase. Your creativity nourishes the seeds you planted. As you reflect on this journey, you draw equilibrium and balance the First Quarter Moon's energy before tipping the scales in your favor. You feel a sense of accomplishment of having made progress on your journey, yet, there is still a long way to go. Pause, take time to contemplate the path ahead, and begin to nurture your sense of perseverance and grit as things have a ways to go.

◗ Waxing Gibbous Moon

Your plans are growing; the devil is in the detail; a meticulous approach lets you achieve the highest result. You may find a boost arrives and gives a shot of can-do energy. It connects you with new information about the path ahead. The Moon is growing, as is your creativity, inspiration, and focus. It is also a time of essential adjustments, streamlining, evaluating goals, and plotting your course towards the final destination. Success is within reach; a final push will get you through. The wind is beneath your wings, a conclusion within reach, and you have the tools at your disposal to achieve your vision.

◑ Full Moon

The Full Moon is when you often reach a successful conclusion. It does bring a bounty that adds to your harvest. Something unexpected often unfolds that transforms your experience. It catches you by surprise, a breath of fresh air; it is a magical time that lets you appreciate what your work has achieved. It is time for communication and sharing thoughts and ideas. It often brings a revelation eliminating new information. The path clears, and you release doubt, anxiety, and tension. It is a therapeutic and healing time that lets you release old energy positively and supportively.

◑ Waning Gibbous (Disseminating) Moon

The Waning gibbous Moon is perfect for release; it allows you to cut away from areas that hold back true potential. You may feel drained as you have worked hard, journeyed long, and are now creating space to return and complete the cycle. It does see tools arrive to support and nourish your spirit. Creating space to channel your energy effectively and cutting away outworn regions creates an environment that lets your ideas and efforts bloom. It is a healing time, a time of acceptance that things move forward towards completing a cycle. This the casting off the outworn, the debris that accumulates over the lunar month is a vital cleansing that clears space and resolves complex emotions that may cling to your energy if not addressed.

Third (Last/Reconciling) Quarter Moon

This Moon is about stabilizing your foundations. There is uncertainty, shifting sands; as change surrounds your life, take time to be mindful of drawing balance into your world. It is the perfect time to reconnect with simple past times and hobbies. Securing and tethering your energy does build a stable foundation from which to grow your world. It is time to take stock and balance areas of your life. Consolidating your power, nurturing your inner child lets you embrace a chapter to focus on the areas that bring you joy. It is not time to advance or acquire new goals. It's a restful phase that speaks of simple pastimes that nurture your spirit.

Waning Crescent (Balsamic) Moon

The Waning Crescent Moon completes the cycle; it is the Moon that finishes the set. It lets you tie up loose ends, finish the finer details, and essentially creates space for new inspiration to flow into your world once the cycle begins again. The word balsamic speaks of healing and attending to areas that feel raw or sensitive. It is a mystical phase that reconnects you to the cycle of life. As the Moon dies away, you can move away from areas that feel best left behind. A focus on healing, meditation, self-care, and nurturing one's spirit is essential during this Moon phase.

Fairy & Pixie Guides

When you harness the power of Fairies and Pixies, you take on their gifts, talents, and abilities. This guide helps you navigate your life adeptly, and it offers you the power of resilience, tenacity, and perseverance. Here is an alphabetical list of channeled Fairies and Pixies in this year's Diary:

Adele is a crusader who fights injustice. Adele loves a mission, a worthy cause to explore. She is an idealist at heart and dedicates herself, compassion, and soul to improving outcomes. She moves forward with determination and carries a great deal of emotional strength within her spirit.

Alice is intense and mesmerizing. She possesses a courageous heart and dives into adventures with a passion. An explorer of the unknown, her curiosity is insatiable. She investigates and delves deeply into new pathways to bring new options to light.

Amber, the Fire Fairy, her energy is smoldering; she simmers with chemistry and character. Amber is an optimistic person with a daring vision to improve the world around her. This Firery Fairy is independent, enquiring, and generous. She is an honest and dependable fairy with an innovative flare. Call on Amber if you need to come up with inspired solutions and achieve dramatic results.

Caitlin is as deep and unfathomable as the ocean. At first approach, she can appear aloof. She is independent, with an extraordinary depth of vision that provides her with intuitive insights. Her enquiring mind is thought-provoking and sharp. She has a darker side to her moods that few get to see. On the surface, she is independent, self-reliant, and adventurous. Her fun-loving attitude seeks freedom and expression.

Chloe, the devil's advocate Fairy, is sweet as angel dust on the insight, yet tough as nails when facing a formidable foe. She has a compelling and noble presence. Chloe is controversial and provocative, willing to debate with others to achieve her point of view. She is expressive, lively, and with the right people, exceptionally loving. Be her friend, and her tenderness will surprise you.

Chrissie is strong-willed, persistent, and meticulous. She is confident, ambitious, and motivated. This Fairy is a natural leader with a strong sense of persuasion, motivating others to join her tribe. She has high standards and a desire to elevate those around her.

Coral is an Ocean dwelling Fairy who speaks up for protecting the world's oceans. She is lively and intelligent, with a bright and sincere manner. She says that when you look below the surface, you get in tune with your deeper feelings. Reflecting on your emotional world is a beautiful harmonizer that brings balance into focus. Nurturing and caring for yourself is the first step in looking after the world and all its inhabitants. We are all interconnected and reliant on each other to care and show compassion.

Danielle is feisty, fun, and vibrant. Danielle possesses a magnetic personality and a well-developed sense of insight and intuition. She is focused, independent, and has impressive persistence in achieving her goals.

Destiny is the fortune-telling Fairy; she is competitive, competent, and goal orientated. Self-assured and independent, Destiny is an authority figure who gives guidance and helps shape your life goals. Destiny is an organizational wizard. Her planning skills make her the go-to Fairy when you have broader life questions in your life. She has a beautiful ability to improve security, and this draws grounded foundations. She is as dependable and protective as any fairy can be.

Ellie is impulsive and pioneering. She dedicates herself to achieving her vision. She has a quick mind and a remarkable memory that is a perfect match for developing innovative endeavors. Call on Ellie when you need to respond to problems with tangible and practical strategies.

Fern is the Green Fairy; she is discreet, adaptable, and pragmatic. She has a charming, chameleon-like quality and can easily blend into her environment. Her gracious and compassionate nature is soothing; she brings balance and harmony into situations. Fern has a unique style and a flair for improving outcomes.

Helena is a bookworm Fairy; she is creative at heart. She is imaginative, intuitive, and understands the value of the written and spoken word. She carries her message through communication, emotions, and concepts. Helena is rational, practical, and her ideas are thought-provoking. She encourages others to share thoughts, feelings, and ideas.

Holly is the Christmas Fairy, who is charming, social, and diplomatic. She has been blessed with impeccable manners and is inherently agreeable. She adds taste and culture to social occasions. Her energy is artistic, harmonious, and friendly. She enriches social events and brings a positive energy that smooths over any uneven edges.

Lily is the Nature Fairy, who has a calming influence that draws balance. Lily is kindhearted, enchanting, and compassionate. She is devoted to others and highly loyal. Her kind, sympathetic nature makes her a natural healer and a fairy you can call upon when you need guidance. There is an aura of prophetic wisdom around Lily that makes her wise and knowing. She is intelligent, insightful, and gifted.

Melody is the Musical Fairy; her tune is calming. She has the temperament of an artistic dreamer; she is graceful, visionary, and deeply spiritual. Her bottomless reservoir of empathy and compassion makes her a natural healer. She is a lover of the creative arts and nurtures her environment with passion. She is selfless and kindhearted. Her generosity always touches the heart of others.

Phoebe, the creatively gifted Fairy is expressive and outspoken; she is a bright star who shines in all she embarks upon growing. To fully thrive, she needs the whole reign of her creativity and vision. She is entrepreneurial, innovative, and expressive. Phoebe makes her mark on the world by using her unique talents to create things she can share with a broader audience. Call on Phoebe when you have a business idea or are moving out of your comfort zone to try something new.

Sienna is a good listener and a persuasive communicator. She is affectionate, playful, and charming. She is talented and a quick thinker with an artistic temperament. Her mental agility enables her to win arguments easily.

Stella is the Psychic Fairy; not much gets past this intelligent Fairy. Ideas and concepts are her forte. She is curious about everything. Flashes of intuition let her use her insight to stunning effect. She possesses innate charm and charisma that attracts others into her sphere. Her grace and kindness radiate outwardly. Stella is romantic, amiable, and compassionate.

Storm is the Thunder and Lightning Fairy. She teaches that while there will always be storms in life, you can endure inclement weather and reach the other side. Storm is flamboyant and joyful; she escapes to far-flung places for the sheer enjoyment of the adventure. She never holds back and dives into new experiences with abandon. She gives you a secure connection with the power of nature. She is a valuable ally to call upon when facing difficulties.

Summer is the warm weather Fairy, who lives for adventures and summer escapades. She is irreverent, entertaining, and youthful. Summer exudes wanderlust and is the perfect companion for picnics and travel. She is an intrepid explorer who encourages the expansion of horizons. Group occasions have enormous appeal; she attracts good friends and values personal bonds. A lover of freedom, Summer explores new frontiers with passion.

Trixie is the Party Fairy, bright, lively, and young at heart; she loves to splash at social events. She is always on the move, intelligent, quick, and fast on the uptake. Her sense of humor is vibrant and expressive. Spirited discussions and thought-provoking chats with friends make Trixie's day.

Vanessa is the circus Fairy who connects us to the carnival of life. She has a freedom-loving, bohemian attitude that sparkles with sweetness. This Fairy loves to travel and see the world. She brightens your environment with an aura that glows with a deep sense of purpose and happiness. Vanessa is affectionate, loving, and creative. She has high regard for people and enjoys entertaining and social occasions. Innately exuberant, she is full of life and commands center stage with her brilliance.

Willow is the flexible Fairy who is kindhearted with a solid affinity for nature and the land. She is creative, artistic, and down-to-earth. Her adaptability makes her a valuable ally who assists you in finding a re-route around problems. Whenever you face a hurdle, don't give up on your dreams; find the solution. Even if it veers you off course, it's likely to take you where you need to go.

Zara is the Stardust Fairy, who reminds you that we are all made from magic. She connects you to the universe and the mysteries of life. Zara is a spontaneous and playful fairy who is highly adaptable. She is young at heart and lightens the mood with her fanciful stories and wanderlust. She dreams big, and her heart encompasses all life. Zara is the ultimate enricher, who is bright and friendly.

Time set to Coordinated Universal Time Zone (UT±0)

I've noted Meteor Showers on the date they peak.

January

Sun	Mon	Tue	Wed	Thu	Fri	Sat
						1
2	3	4	5	6	7	8
9	10	11	12	13	14	15
16	17	18	19	20	21	22
23	24	25	26	27	28	29
30	31					

January Astrology

2ND - NEW MOON IN CAPRICORN 18:33

3RD - QUADRANTIDS METEOR SHOWER. JANUARY 1ST-5TH.

7TH - MERCURY AT GREATEST EASTERN ELONGATION

9TH - FIRST QUARTER MOON IN ARIES 18:11

14TH - MERCURY RETROGRADE BEGINS IN AQUARIUS

17TH - WOLF MOON. FULL MOON IN CANCER 23:48

25TH - LAST QUARTER MOON SCORPIO 13:42

NEW MOON

WOLF MOON

31 Friday

1 Saturday ~ New Year's Day

2 Sunday ~ New Moon in Capricorn 18:33

Fairy Amber shares that there is a greater emphasis on your home life at this time. It links you up to an enterprising and creative chapter that enables you to grow your talents. It lets you create space to tackle those projects which have been on the backburner. It brings helpful distractions as you immerse yourself in nurturing your abilities. It brings a sense of well-being that marks a unique path forward. It brings opportunities to use your skills and enjoy focusing on the basics in your life. A social aspect opens the door to a group event soon. It is a time of social outings and expansion. It transitions you forward and closes the door on the past.

3 Monday ~ Quadrantids Meteor Shower runs Jan 1 – 5

4 Tuesday

5 Wednesday

6 Thursday

7 Friday ~ Mercury at Greatest Eastern Elongation

8 Saturday

9 Sunday ~ First Quarter Moon in Aries 18:11

Chrissie says that an entrepreneurial aspect ahead gives you opportunities to grow a fascinating path forward. It brings an extended time where you utilize inherent skills and draws security into your world. It brings a grounded environment that helps you develop a promising area. It may have you rethinking long-term plans as a new trajectory calls your name. It takes you to a radiant time of nurturing your gifts of creativity and innovation. It brings magic and growth, which kickstarts a refreshing time of expanding your world as you pour your energy into a worthwhile area.

10 Monday

11 Tuesday

12 Wednesday

13 Thursday

14 Friday ~ Mercury Retrograde begins in Aquarius

15 Saturday

16 Sunday

Fairy Phoebe shares that nurturing creativity and experimenting with new pathways bring excitement to the forefront of your life. Have fun exploring refreshing options and see what grows. Your intuition helps guide you towards an opportunity that has room to develop your abilities. It brings a busy and active time of using your talents and getting involved with new endeavors. A highly productive chapter becomes a source of inspiration that draws change into your world. It leads down a path that progresses your skills and elevates prospects. It revolutionizes your circumstances and lets you reap the rewards of expanding your abilities into new areas. It brings a busy and active time of development and learning.

17 Monday ~ Martin Luther King Day
Full Moon in Cancer 23:48
Wolf Moon

18 Tuesday

19 Wednesday

20 Thursday

21 Friday

22 Saturday

23 Sunday

Fairy Destiny says to beware of making any rash decisions. You could waste a good amount of energy on something that muddies the waters and gets you bogged down in a complicated arena. Old challenging issues may surface, reigniting insights into your life and past agreements. As the shadow of old thinking casts doubt on the potential possible, you are wise to keep open to new opportunities that arrive to tempt you forward. Your hunches play an essential part in discovering new leads. Trusting your instincts and acting on clear insights restores the flow of potential in your life. It carries you through challenges and lets you find the safe harbor of smooth sailing.

24 Monday

25 Tuesday ~ Last Quarter Moon Scorpio 13:42

26 Wednesday

27 Thursday

28 Friday

29 Saturday

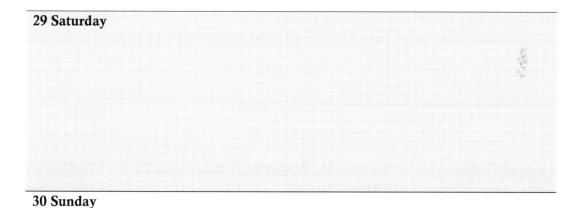

30 Sunday

Fairy Amber says that news arrives that brings excitement into your life. It has you feeling optimistic about rising prospects that bring new options. It leads to a time that pushes back boundaries and overcomes the limitations as you dive deep into developing your vision. A unique landscape tempts you forward as your imagination ignites with fresh inspiration. Priorities and plans soon take shape. As your vision takes form and creativity heightens, your enthusiasm and motivation bring great excitement. It fuels options that improve your social life. Getting involved with others with similar goals can contribute ideas and thoughts and bring value to your life.

FEBRUARY

Sun	Mon	Tue	Wed	Thu	Fri	Sat
		1	2	3	4	5
6	7	8	9	10	11	12
13	14	15	16	17	18	19
20	21	22	23	24	25	26
27	28					

February Astrology

1st - New Moon in Aquarius 05:45

1st - Chinese New Year (Tiger)

1st - Imbolc

4th - Mercury Retrograde ends in Capricorn

8th - First Quarter Moon in Taurus 13:50

16th - Mercury at Greatest Western Elongation

16th - Snow Moon. Full Moon in Leo 16:57

23rd - Last Quarter Moon in Scorpio 22:32

_____

_____

_____

_____

_____

_____

New Moon

SNOW MOON

31 Monday

1 Tuesday ~ New Moon in Aquarius 05:45
Chinese New Year (Tiger)
Imbolc

2 Wednesday~ Groundhog Day

3 Thursday

4 Friday ~ Mercury Retrograde ends in Capricorn

5 Saturday

6 Sunday

Caitlin says that you soon make good headway around developing your goals. It brings a lucky break that you have worked hard to accomplish. A door opens towards advancing your life into a prestigious new area. A focused effort to improve your circumstances draws dividends. It lets you navigate a complex strategy and come out on top. Developments ahead allow the pieces of your puzzle to fall into place, setting the stage to nurture your abilities. Refining and tweaking your talents puts you on track to obtain a successful outcome. You dive into a new role soon, and this brings bustling activity. Improving your life is a big theme. It sets the stage for a productive chapter that revolutionizes your outlook.

7 Monday

8 Tuesday ~ First Quarter Moon in Taurus 13:50

9 Wednesday

10 Thursday

11 Friday

12 Saturday

13 Sunday

Adele shares that a brighter world of opportunity is ready to emerge in your life. You reveal an exciting avenue that offers a curious sideline for your creative inspiration. It captures the essence of dreams, hopes, and joy. Developing your vision draws a happy time to work with your abilities and merge ideas with others on a similar trajectory. Unleashing your skills in a broader arena of potential brings fascinating opportunities to grow your talents. It lets you forge new friends and connect with people who nurture your creativity. A gateway ahead brings a journey of excitement and adventure. It turns up the potential as your life transforms into a productive and active environment. It helps you branch out and explore uncharted territory.

14 Monday ~ Valentine's Day

15 Tuesday

16 Wednesday ~ Mercury at Greatest Western Elongation
Full Moon in Leo 16:57
Snow Moon.

17 Thursday

18 Friday

19 Saturday

20 Sunday

Trixie says that change surrounds your life. It brings a chance to nurture a bond that offers a new page of potential. Pouring your energy into a path that holds meaning sees you shift your focus to developing a bond. Inspiration flows into your life, restoring balance. This person has a big personality that lights up your world. Full of happiness and sunshine, they are supportive, creative, and confident. They are a radiant and hearty person with a good sense of humor. This person is magnetic with a powerful presence. They have a focused sense of purpose and the determination to embrace challenges. You find it is easy to initiate a closer bond with this person this week.

21 Monday ~ Presidents' Day

22 Tuesday

23 Wednesday ~ Last Quarter Moon in Scorpio 22:32

24 Thursday

25 Friday

26 Saturday

27 Sunday

Alice reveals that a generous offer makes itself known soon. It allows you to work with your abilities, which rules a path that sweeps in new potential. It places you in the box seat to evolve your skills and refine your talents. It represents a new beginning that marks the start of a dynamic phase that is inspired and purposeful. It brings growth and productivity as expansion comes calling. It lets you secure new possibilities that draw grounded foundations into your environment. It allows improvement to open the door to progressing your larger goals. The more you nurture your life, the more you discover talents that are ready to shine. Getting involved with a group environment adds fuel to your motivation. It brings the inspiration to expand your horizons.

MARCH

Sun	Mon	Tue	Wed	Thu	Fri	Sat
		1	2	3	4	5
6	7	8	9	10	11	12
13	14	15	16	17	18	19
20	21	22	23	24	25	26
27	28					

March Astrology

2nd - New Moon in Pisces 17:34

10th - First Quarter Moon in Gemini 10:45

18th - Worm Moon. Full Moon in Virgo 07:17

20th - Ostara/Spring Equinox 15:33

25th - Last Quarter Moon in Capricorn 05:37

NEW MOON

WORM MOON

_____

_____

_____

_____

_____

_____

_____

28 Monday

1 Tuesday Shrove ~ Tuesday (Mardi Gras)

2 Wednesday ~ Ash Wednesday Lent Begins
New Moon in Pisces 17:34

3 Thursday

4 Friday

5 Saturday

6 Sunday

Zara is excited to share that you uncover new information when a conversation flips your world upside down. It is open, authentic, and spoken from the heart. It brings a time for building bonds and opening potential for your social life. It draws stabilizing energy that heightens well-being and lights a path towards positive communication and shared experiences. It places you in a prime alignment to enjoy abundance as you solidify foundations and move towards developing your life. It brings opportunities to socialize as the path forward appears and things fall into place. An endeavor you become involved with dials up with new possibilities. It opens the door towards progressing a dream.

7 Monday

8 Tuesday

9 Wednesday

10 Thursday ~ First Quarter Moon in Gemini 10:45

11 Friday

12 Saturday

13 Sunday

Melody says that an enchanting chapter brings a shift forward that directs your energy towards a path that offers room to grow your life. It plants the seeds for an exciting journey to unfold. Mingling with your circle of friends brings heightened activity and invitations. New potential sweeps in, moving you forward towards a stable chapter of growing your social life. It brings a slow and steady transformation that offers personal growth and connection. A more social environment ahead generates new possibilities for your life. Being open and flexible to new people does set the tone for an influx of potential. Your social life moves towards a more active environment, creating the perfect conditions to connect with .magic.

14 Monday

15 Tuesday

16 Wednesday ~ Purim (Begins at sundown)

17 Thursday ~ Purim (Ends at sunset)
St Patrick's Day

18 Friday ~ Full Moon in Virgo 07:17

19 Saturday

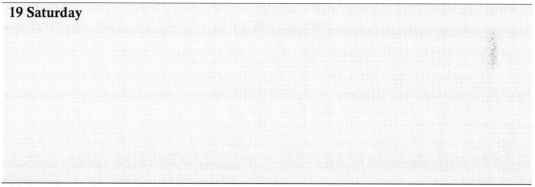

20 Sunday ~ Ostara/Spring Equinox 15:33

Alice says that you soon gain insight into the path ahead. It brings an opportunity that lets you step into your power and achieve a magnificent result. It brings new options that keep life humming along sustainably and progressively. It sets the stage to develop a situation that inspires change. The borders of your life expand and give you an exciting glimpse of future possibilities. In the pipeline, you discover an area worth your time; it offers a new level of advancement that captures the essence of prosperity and growth. Making your mark on the world brings profound change. It aligns you correctly and lets you take advantage of an offer that crops up. It gives you the green light to expand your horizons and discover new areas of potential.

21 Monday

22 Tuesday

23 Wednesday

24 Thursday

25 Friday ~ Last Quarter Moon in Capricorn 05:37

26 Saturday

27 Sunday

Fairy Danielle says that creating space to nurture priorities brings a comforting sense of security on the home front. Little routines bless your life, and you soon remedy restlessness with new choices and opportunities. It draws balance into your life and creates a shift towards positive emotions. It helps bring an enterprising idea to fruition. Earthy harmonies offer grounding energy that generates greater ease in all you do. Releasing outworn energy removes tension and balances stress. It draws equilibrium into your foundations. Implementing grounding practices creates a firm basis from which to improve your circumstances. Extra opportunities ahead open the gates to a busy and productive chapter. Surprise news lights the path forward.

28 Monday

29 Tuesday

30 Wednesday

31 Thursday

APRIL

Sun	Mon	Tue	Wed	Thu	Fri	Sat
					1	2
3	4	5	6	7	8	9
10	11	12	13	14	15	16
17	18	19	20	21	22	23
24	25	26	27	28	29	30

April Astrology

1st - New Moon in Aries 06:24

9th - First Quarter Moon in Cancer 06:47

16th - Pink Moon. Full Moon in Libra 18:54

22nd - Lyrids Meteor Shower from April 16-25

23rd - Last Quarter Moon in Aquarius 11:56.

29th - Mercury Greatest Eastern Elongation of 20.6 degrees from the Sun.

30th - New Moon in Taurus 20:27

_____

_____

_____

_____

_____

_____

NEW MOON

_____

_____

_____

_____

_____

_____

_____

PINK MOON

APRIL

1 Friday ~ All Fools/April Fool's Day
New Moon in Aries 06:24

2 Saturday ~ Ramadan Begins

3 Sunday

Summer shares that it shows a time that brims with potential. It gives you a leg up on an environment that offers stability and growth. It helps you head towards developing your life outwardly. It grows creativity and advances your abilities into a new area. It turns out to be worth your time as you initiate a project that draws magic into your world. Focusing on developing your life offers a worthwhile mission. The good news is coming soon, and you have worked hard to achieve this result. Life is ready to shower new possibilities into your world. Examining the path ahead brings a journey worth developing. It does grow your skills in critical areas.

4 Monday

5 Tuesday

6 Wednesday

7 Thursday

8 Friday

9 Saturday ~ First Quarter Moon in Cancer 06:47

10 Sunday ~ Palm Sunday.

Phoebe shares that an opportunity arrives that sets the stage for new ideas to flourish. It offers an excellent ripple effect that outwardly expands your life. It brings a lucky break that helps you launch into a journey that inspires and motivates growth. Themes of abundance, security, and happiness soon emerge in your life. It ratchets up the potential and lets you push back the barriers as you dive in towards a new chapter of potential. It does have you thinking about the future in a new light. Taking time to draw balance and equilibrium into your environment provides the right music to your soul. It is a time that sees new possibilities shining.

11 Monday

12 Tuesday

13 Wednesday

14 Thursday ~ Lent Ends

15 Friday ~ Passover (begins at sunset)
Good Friday

16 Saturday ~ Full Moon in Libra 18:54
Pink Moon

17 Sunday ~Easter Sunday

Vanessa shares news arrives soon that sparks evolution in your life. It marks a refreshing time that rules expansion in your social circle. Life sprinkles new possibilities that, when nurtured, offer a chance to bloom. It is the continuation of a more comprehensive theme of change that surrounds your life. Sweeping away outworn areas creates space to focus on nurturing dreams. An attractive viewpoint comes into view and touches you down on an exciting landscape of unique options. It brings a happy time that captures the essence of excitement. Your willingness to push back boundaries is fundamental in achieving growth. It does bring options that you would not ordinarily discover.

18 Monday

19 Tuesday

20 Wednesday

21 Thursday

22 Friday ~ Lyrids Meteor Shower from April 16-25
Passover (ends at sunset)
Orthodox Good Friday
Earth Day

23 Saturday ~ Last Quarter Moon in Aquarius 11:56

24 Sunday ~ Orthodox Easter

Fairy Willow reveals that new options are coming soon that shifts your focus towards developing an enterprising area. It brings a project that offers a social aspect. A creative journey beckons your heart. It lets you work with your talents and immerse yourself in a productive environment. It glides you towards a relaxing scene that nurtures well-being and favors expansion in your social life. It places you well to improve your circumstances when new information reaches you. It brings a forward-facing chapter to light that offers progression. A plethora of new possibilities opens the gate on an exciting path. Changes flow into your world that draws a stable environment. There is something on offer soon that makes the most of your abilities.

25 Monday

26 Tuesday

27 Wednesday

28 Thursday

MAY

Sun	Mon	Tue	Wed	Thu	Fri	Sat
1	2	3	4	5	6	7
8	9	10	11	12	13	14
15	16	17	18	19	20	21
22	23	24	25	26	27	28
29	30	31				

MAY ASTROLOGY

6TH - ETA AQUARIDS METEOR SHOWER, APRIL 19TH - MAY 28TH

9TH - FIRST QUARTER MOON IN LEO 00:21

10TH - MERCURY RETROGRADE BEGINS IN GEMINI

16TH - TOTAL LUNAR ECLIPSE 01:32

16TH - FLOWER MOON. FULL MOON IN SCORPIO 04:13

22ND - LAST QUARTER MOON IN AQUARIUS 18:43

30TH - NEW QUARTER MOON IN LEO 00:21

_____

_____

_____

_____

_____

_____

_____

NEW MOON

FLOWER MOON

---

29 Friday ~ Mercury Greatest Eastern Elongation of 20.6 degrees from the Sun.

30 Saturday ~ Partial Solar Eclipse
New Moon in Taurus 20:27

1 Sunday ~ Beltane/May Day
Ramadan Ends

Helena shares that setting aspirations is a decisive step forward that helps you explore new opportunities. A theme of abundance, security, and renewal supports your growth and evolution. Being proactive lets you discover a journey that speaks to your heart. It unfurls new possibilities that spring to life a glorious chapter that nurtures creativity and balances foundations. Exciting changes are coming up for you. It does see activity buzzing around the broader circle of your friends. It brings an invitation that supports well-being and a practical sense of connection with those you enjoy spending time with kindred folk. It draws a path that offers rejuvenation and happiness. It brings a time of lively discussions, collaboration, and teamwork.

MAY

2 Monday

3 Tuesday

4 Wednesday

5 Thursday

6 Friday ~ Eta Aquarids Meteor Shower April 19th - May 28th

7 Saturday

8 Sunday ~ Mother's Day

The Fairies speak of improvement coming; it relates to advancing your situation forward. It creates space to nurture your skills and get involved in an area that captures the essence of creativity. Imagination and inspiration run wild as you attract new possibilities into your life. It brings a vital phase that offers lighter energy. Funneling your skills into an area that provides progression draws impressive results. Your life is ripe with potential that is just waiting to blossom. It brings a time of increasing stability that marks an energizing chapter. As you expand your vision, you take a highly productive path that offers growth and expansion.

MAY

9 Monday ~ First Quarter Moon in Leo 00:21

10 Tuesday ~ Mercury Retrograde begins in Gemini.

11 Wednesday

12 Thursday

13 Friday

14 Saturday

15 Sunday

Willow sensitively shares that while some days are up and others down during the Mercury Retrograde phase. Overall, you gain traction on a more stable and abundant landscape. You are doing better as fundamental changes occur, which bring a stable and grounded environment that improves your circumstances. A richly creative process is at the crux of this journey; exploring new pathways brings possibilities to contemplate. Working with your abilities and refines talents and improves your life from the ground up. A wave of fresh potential draws rejuvenation. You harness a rebel's instinct and discover new pathways towards growth. It brings a freewheeling and wild chapter that tempts you forward.

16 Monday ~ Full Moon in Scorpio 04:13
Total Lunar Eclipse 01:32
Flower Moon

17 Tuesday

18 Wednesday

19 Thursday

20 Friday

21 Saturday

22 Sunday ~ Last Quarter Moon in Aquarius 18:43

Coral shares that sensitive emotions can arise from a tendency to self-sabotage. Be mindful of your thoughts; you have the strength of heart to enter a cycle that stirs creative juices and illuminates new possibilities. Realigning your energies draws balance, and this supports a contented rhythm that re-emerges in your world. It leads towards a productive chapter that reawakens and animates your life. A change of orientation brings excitement that is a perfect remedy. A new adventure calls your name, and this removes the restrictions that have limited progress. It draws an adventurous chapter of liberation, freedom, and expansion.

23 Monday ~ Victoria Day (Canada)

24 Tuesday

25 Wednesday

26 Thursday

MAY

27 Friday

28 Saturday

29 Sunday

Sienna says that you enter an extended time that donates essential changes, bringing a fantastic boost into your life. It helps heal the old wounds that prevent progress. It gets time with supportive people who nurture your spirit. Creating space to promote new possibilities brings a windfall of refreshing options. Socialising, mingling, and sharing ideas offer a chapter that fosters creativity and balances emotions. The time is right to move forward. You turn a corner, and this brings more stability. Indeed, re-balancing your feelings even the playing field. It prepares your foundations to expand into new areas.

JUNE

Sun	Mon	Tue	Wed	Thu	Fri	Sat
			1	2	3	4
5	6	7	8	9	10	11
12	13	14	15	16	17	18
19	20	21	22	23	24	25
26	27	28	29	30		

June Astrology

3rd - Mercury Retrograde ends in Taurus

7th - First Quarter Moon in Virgo 14:48

14th - Strawberry Moon. Full Moon in Sagittarius Supermoon 11:51

16th - Mercury's greatest Western elongation of 23.2 degrees from the Sun

21st - Last Quarter Moon in Aries 03:11

21st - Midsummer/Litha Solstice 09:13

29th - New Moon in Cancer 02:52

_____

_____

_____

_____

_____

_____

NEW MOON

_____

_____

_____

_____

_____

_____

_____

STRAWBERRY MOON

30 Monday ~ New Moon in Gemini 11:30
Memorial Day

31 Tuesday

1 Wednesday

2 Thursday

3 Friday ~ Mercury Retrograde ends in Taurus

4 Saturday ~ Shavuot (Begins at sunset)

5 Sunday

Chloe explains that by moving away from restlessness and anxiety that saps energy, you can use your gift of humor to resolve tricky situations. A genuine and timely shift is well supported, and this opens your life to new people and possibilities. The choices you make help get the balance right in your life. Unpredictable currents may create uncertainty, but these mark a significant point of realization that gives you insight into your future direction. Setting intentions lets you take the first step towards your dream destination. Getting involved in an area that holds your focus brings a valuable sense of connection and abundance. It places you in a zone where things flow naturally along.

6 Monday ~ Shavuot (Ends at sunset)

7 Tuesday ~ First Quarter Moon in Virgo 14:48

8 Wednesday

9 Thursday

10 Friday

11 Saturday

12 Sunday

Fairy Vanessa says that news arrives that brings change and opportunity. It offers a shift forward that opens the path ahead. Taking advantage of new potential puts you in the prime position to draw an influx of good fortune into your world. It leads towards developing hopes and dreams as an expansive arena comes into view. It offers a busy time that lets you move up the ladder of success. It marks a bold beginning that brings joy and harmony into view. An abundant mindset broadens the playing field and draws brainstorming sessions with kindred spirits. It gets an upgrade to your life that offers room to progress goals.

13 Monday

14 Tuesday ~ Full Moon in Sagittarius, Supermoon 11:51
Strawberry Moon.
Flag Day

15 Wednesday

16 Thursday ~ Mercury's greatest Western elongation of 23.2 degrees from the Sun

17 Friday

18 Saturday

19 Sunday ~ Father's Day

Willow is pleased to share that you uncover a piece of confidential information that cracks the code to a more expansive social life. Abundant properties blossom. Blending these elements lets you craft a path that is in alignment with your vision for future growth. An opportunity comes knocking that offers a chance to spread your wings in a new area. It is the catalyst for change that shifts your focus forward towards an enterprising area. It leads to a busy and productive environment that gives you the green light to enjoy life. Change flows into your world, and this sweeps away the cobwebs. It brings a chance to socialize with friends and mingle in your broader community. It sets the stage for an expressive and happy time spent with friends.

20 Monday

21 Tuesday ~ Midsummer/Litha Solstice. 09:13
Last Quarter Moon in Aries 03:11

22 Wednesday

23 Thursday

24 Friday

25 Saturday

26 Sunday

Zara reveals that life offers pearls of wisdom that give you insight into a deeper reality. It provides access to more profound truths that creates space to nurture a spiritual path. It brings an enriching time of developing your talents and immersing yourself in an area of interest. It draws stability that marks a turning point as it underscores a time of change that supports meaning and growth in your life. It lets you plug into a path that aligns with destiny—hearing the call of the wild sparks an engaging time of exploring wisdom. Nurturing your dreams draws positive influences that let you get in touch with your higher calling. It brings a positive note that enables you to develop your life in alignment with your vision. Your intuition is instrumental in guiding the path ahead.

27 Monday

28 Tuesday

29 Wednesday ~ New Moon in Cancer 02:52

30 Thursday

July

Sun	Mon	Tue	Wed	Thu	Fri	Sat
					1	2
3	4	5	6	7	8	9
10	11	12	13	14	15	16
17	18	19	20	21	22	23
24	25	26	27	28	29	30

July Astrology

7TH - First Quarter Moon in Libra 02:14

13TH - Buck Moon. Full Moon in Capricorn. Supermoon 18:37

20TH - Last Quarter Moon in Aries 14:18

28TH - New Moon in Leo 17:54

28TH - Delta Aquarids Meteor Shower. July 12th - August 23rd

NEW MOON

BUCK MOON

1 Friday ~ Canada Day

2 Saturday

3 Sunday

Fairy Alice shares that your priorities are shifting; it brings a journey that develops your world. Your situation is transforming towards a busy and creative time of working with your abilities. It helps you shift away from areas that no longer inspire or hold water. Pouring your energy into a journey worth growing brings change that guides your progress forward. It governs a time of increasing stability that rules getting back to basics and working with your skills to advance life. It grounds your energy in an environment that is ripe with potential ready to grow.

4 Monday ~ Independence Day

5 Tuesday

6 Wednesday

7 Thursday ~ First Quarter Moon in Libra 02:14

8 Friday

9 Saturday

10 Sunday

Storm reveals that researching options will provide a passageway towards growth. Visionary ideas heighten creativity and bring a turning point to your life. You move towards developing an area that captures interest. It underscores the energy of magic available when you expand your life outwardly. Life soon bustles with lighter energy; the pace is progressive. It brings a productive cycle that fuels new growth. **It** gets exciting developments that lead to new possibilities. It involves a social aspect that draws thoughtful conversations, good company, and social expansion—exploring your options jumpstarts a fresh track forward. It does have you sharing new adventures with an engaging companion. You become more confident about going after your goals.

11 Monday

12 Tuesday

13 Wednesday ~ Full Moon in Capricorn, Supermoon 18:37
Buck Moon

14 Thursday

15 Friday

16 Saturday

17 Sunday

Your fairy guides say you can expect extra opportunities ahead that nurture a sense of self-expression. It brings a creative aspect that builds a path of increasing stability. It releases uncertainty and lets you immerse your energy in an area that captures the essence of manifestation. It brings fullness and fertility to your creativity, bringing new options to contemplate. It offers a peak season for innovation, growth, and good luck. An option ahead becomes a good fit for your life. It brings an opportunity to grow and learn. Your energy moves from strength to strength as you become adept at achieving your goals. Something new is in the pipeline, and when it lands, it brings great excitement. Further information shines a light on advancing your vision

18 Monday

19 Tuesday

20 Wednesday ~ Last Quarter Moon in Aries 14:18

21 Thursday

22 Friday

23 Saturday

24 Sunday

Helena shares that news arrives that helps craft your vision for future growth. It begins a journey that advances your life towards new options. It marks a significant turning point that lets you take hold of the reins and take charge of developing your life. It brings a lovely boost as lighter energy offers heightened inspiration and motivation. Creativity rises, delivering a wellspring of possibilities. Inspiration and creativity are running rife through this dynamic environment. It brings a social aspect that involves lively conversations and enthusiastic discussions. It does have you opening the door to an expressive path that draws enrichment and abundance into your world.

25 Monday

26 Tuesday

27 Wednesday

28 Thursday ~ Delta Aquarids Meteor Shower. July 12th – August 23rd
New Moon in Leo 17:54

29 Friday ~ Islamic New Year

30 Saturday

31 Sunday

Fairy Summer advises that alchemy is brewing in the background of your life that brings new options. Refining and streamlining your life draws an effective and efficient path towards growing your world. It brings good fortune and improvement to your social life when a chance collaboration inspires growth and progression. It broadens your perception of what is possible when you open your life to new people and experiences. Getting involved in developing goals helps manifest a cycle of success. It highlights growing your abilities and extending your reach as you advance towards a lofty goal.

AUGUST

Sun	Mon	Tue	Wed	Thu	Fri	Sat
	1	2	3	4	5	6
7	8	9	10	11	12	13
14	15	16	17	18	19	20
21	22	23	24	25	26	27
28	29	30	31			

August Astrology

5th - First Quarter Moon Scorpio 11:06

8th - Full Moon in Aquarius Supermoon 01:35. Sturgeon Moon.

8th - Perseids Meteor Shower July 17th - August 24th

14th - Saturn at Opposition

19th - Last Quarter Moon in Taurus 04:36

27th - New Moon in Virgo 08:16

27th - Mercury at Greatest Eastern Elongation at 27.3 degrees from the Sun

_____

_____

_____

_____

_____

_____

NEW MOON

STURGEON MOON

_____

_____

_____

_____

_____

_____

_____

1 Monday ~ Lammas/Lughnasadh

2 Tuesday

3 Wednesday

4 Thursday

5 Friday ~ First Quarter Moon Scorpio 11:06

6 Saturday

7 Sunday

Caitlin reveals that taking inventory of your situation helps pinpoint areas for removal. It brings an optimistic phase that lets you make headway on planning for future growth. It opens the floodgates towards an enterprising avenue that brings an active and vibrant chapter of working towards your goals. It helps you sidestep roadblocks and open a path that offers progress and prosperity. It brings an energetic rhythm that is dynamic and inspired. Embracing new experiences widens the borders of your life. Getting a fresh start inspires your mind and illuminates new options. It draws lighter energy, and a fresh wind of possibility helps you soar to new heights.

8 Monday

9 Tuesday

10 Wednesday

11 Thursday

12 Friday ~ Perseids Meteor Shower July 17th - August 24th
Full Moon in Aquarius, Supermoon 01:35
Sturgeon Moon

13 Saturday

14 Sunday ~ Saturn at Opposition

Your fairy guides speak of a time of self-discovery ahead that opens the floodgates to a happier chapter. Indeed, harnessing the magic in your world is a fantastic way to increase the inspiration in your world. It opens the path towards rising abundance. It liberates your mood with a freedom-loving journey that offers an influx of options to tempt you towards growth. The essence of manifestation gently weaves a soul journey through your life. Expanding your horizons lets you seek opportunities that enable you to grow your talents. It plants the seeds for future growth. You can look forward to a refreshing change of pace.

15 Monday

16 Tuesday

17 Wednesday

18 Thursday

19 Friday ~ Last Quarter Moon in Taurus 04:36

20 Saturday

21 Sunday

Pixie Chrissie says that moving out of your comfort zone draws a pleasing result for your life. It connects you with a social environment that lets you share thoughts and ideas with a kindred spirit. A willingness to be open to new people and possibilities brings a lot happening in your life. It begins a path that nurtures harmony and abundance in your world. Further information lands at your doorstep. It kicks off a social aspect, and life is a whirlwind of fun adventures. Life brings people into your life that understand you on a deeper level. It connects you with your tribe in the most advantageous manner.

22 Monday

23 Tuesday

24 Wednesday

25 Thursday

26 Friday

27 Saturday ~ Mercury at Greatest Eastern Elongation at 27.3 degrees from the Sun
New Moon in Virgo 08:16

28 Sunday

Fairy Storm shares that releasing your troubles to the universe cleans the slate. It heralds a positively charged new beginning. Dusting off underutilized abilities, you sharpen your focus and get busy on a path that inspires your spirit. It draws reinvention and lets you remove elements that are no longer relevant. Life brings new possibilities to light. Your willingness to explore avenues of growth brings new potential flowing into your life. It sparks a big reveal that expands your life outwardly. A promising chapter ahead reshuffle the decks of possibility in your life as you open a gateway forward. A great deal of creativity flows in, sparking significant change.

SEPTEMBER

Sun	Mon	Tue	Wed	Thu	Fri	Sat
				1	2	3
4	5	6	7	8	9	10
11	12	13	14	15	16	17
18	19	20	21	22	23	24
25	26	27	28	29	30	

September Astrology

7TH - FIRST QUARTER MOON SAGITTARIUS 18:08

10TH - MERCURY RETROGRADE BEGINS IN LIBRA

10TH - CORN MOON. HARVEST MOON. FULL MOON IN PISCES 09:58

16TH - NEPTUNE AT OPPOSITION

17TH - LAST QUARTER MOON IN GEMINI 21:52

23 - MABON/FALL EQUINOX. 01:03

25TH - NEW MOON IN LIBRA 21:54

26TH - JUPITER AT OPPOSITION

NEW MOON

Corn/Harvest Moon

_____

_____

_____

_____

_____

_____

_____

29 Monday

30 Tuesday

31 Wednesday

1 Thursday

2 Friday

3 Saturday ~ First Quarter Moon Sagittarius 18:08

4 Sunday

Caitlin reveals that a compelling journey awaits you. Indeed, new options ahead bring the green light to network and expand your circle of friends. It draws a time that nurtures well-being as it brings the music into your world. It puts you in sync with others, which draws a valuable sense of well-being and connection. You find your sense of balance in a new arena and soon generate lively discussions that inspire growth. It brings reinvention and rejuvenation into your life. It puts you in the proper alignment to take advantage of new possibilities that connect you with joy.

5 Monday ~ Labor Day

6 Tuesday

7 Wednesday

8 Thursday

9 Friday

10 Saturday ~ Mercury Retrograde begins in Libra.
Full Moon in Pisces 09:58
Corn Moon. Harvest Moon

11 Sunday

Fairy Destiny is excited to share that unique options are ready to blossom in your world. It speaks about news arriving which takes the edge off your stress levels. It heightens your ability to manifest possibilities. In a nutshell, lighter options emerge to tempt you forward. It draws a time of lively discussions and hatching ideas with kindred spirits. It opens the door to a unique path of connection and growth. It helps break old patterns as you pick up the leads of a new journey that offers expansion. Fulfillment and happiness run rife through this brighter chapter of possibility. You create magic with the options that flow into your life.

12 Monday

13 Tuesday

14 Wednesday

15 Thursday

16 Friday ~ Neptune at Opposition

17 Saturday ~ Last Quarter Moon in Gemini 21:52

18 Sunday

Stella says that this week is a lovely time to create space for nurturing your goals. You touch down on an exciting path that offers new experiences and opportunities. It blazes a creative trail towards using your abilities and refining your talents. Raw potential soon transforms into mastery as you reveal a purposeful and dynamic journey that brings an enterprising chapter ahead. It touches you down on a branch that draws enrichment and joy into your life. The new information ahead provides you with a path that you can progress forward. It brings a transition that lets you enter a new chapter of possibility.

19 Monday

20 Tuesday

21 Wednesday~ International Day of Peace

22 Thursday

23 Friday ~ Mabon/Fall Equinox. 01:03

24 Saturday

25 Sunday ~ Rosh Hashanah (begins at sunset)
New Moon in Libra 21:54

Pixie Helena says that something new emerges that has you learning the ropes. Finding an unfamiliar environment does let you grow your skills in a new area. It brings a time of change that leads to an awakening. New options arrive that unpack additional opportunities to work with your abilities and refine your talents. It shifts your attention to a clear path that offers a pleasing result for your life. It drives your potential forward and gives you a chance to shine in a new area. The wheels are in motion; essential changes occur that offer blessings on several levels. It brings a breath of fresh air into your surroundings and has you feeling renewed.

26 Monday ~ Jupiter at Opposition

27 Tuesday ~ Rosh Hashanah (ends at sunset)

28 Wednesday

29 Thursday

OCTOBER

Sun	Mon	Tue	Wed	Thu	Fri	Sat
						1
2	3	4	5	6	7	8
9	10	11	12	13	14	15
16	17	18	19	20	21	22
23	24	25	26	27	28	29
30	31					

October Astrology

2nd - Mercury Retrograde ends in Virgo

3rd - First Quarter Moon in Capricorn 00.14

7th - Draconids Meteor Shower. Oct 6th-10th

8th - Mercury Greatest Western Elongation

9th - Hunters Moon. Full Moon in Aries 20:54

17th - Last Quarter Moon in Cancer 17.15

21st - Orionids Meteor Shower. October 2nd - November 7th

25th - New Moon in Scorpio 10:48

25th - Partial Solar Eclipse

New Moon

Hunters Moon

30 Friday

1 Saturday

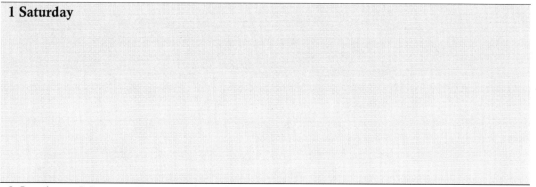

2 Sunday ~ Mercury Retrograde ends in Virgo

Lily says that life brings a considerable boost that opens the door to a path worth following. It brings a focus on developing stable foundations. An emphasis on nurturing your goals lets you come up with a winner. Keeping your eye on the target brings a cycle that leads you towards a prosperous chapter. More balance and harmony emerge, creating the right environment for life to blossom. It brings a good time to trust your instincts and reach for your dreams. It lets you enter a journey that brings refreshing goals into focus. As you mark out the stepping-stones ahead, you discover a significant change. It does bring transformation that sees sunnier skies emerging overhead.

3 Monday ~ First Quarter Moon in Capricorn 00.14

4 Tuesday ~ Yom Kippur (begins at sunset)

5 Wednesday ~ Yom Kippur (ends at sunset)

6 Thursday

7 Friday ~ Draconids Meteor Shower. Oct 6 -10

8 Saturday ~ Mercury Greatest Western Elongation

9 Sunday ~ Sukkot (begins at sunset)
Full Moon in Aries 20:54
Hunters Moon

Fairy Coral shares that an area you become interested in soon shows a great deal of promise. It transitions your focus to a chapter that offers room to see creativity blossom. It lays the foundations for improvement in your home circumstances. Unique opportunities crop up to encourage refining skills and using your inherent abilities. It rules a time of firing up creative skills and enjoying new areas that advance goals. It nurtures a strong foundation from which to grow your life. It underscores the energy of abundance that surrounds your circumstances.

10 Monday ~ Thanksgiving Day (Canada)
Indigenous People's Day
Columbus Day

11 Tuesday

12 Wednesday

13 Thursday

14 Friday

15 Saturday

16 Sunday ~ Sukkot (ends at sunset)

Fairy Willow shares that you turn a corner and navigate the path ahead with grace and flexibility. It lets you invest your energy wisely in improving the circumstances in your life. It links you with kindred spirits who offer support and thoughtful conversations. It brings a time of nurturing many interests and curiosities. Life becomes smoother as you untangle the knots that disrupt your life. It brings a harmonizing aspect that offers lighter energy moving forward. Changes ahead chart a busy and active journey forward. As you draw abundance, you create foundations that provide room to grow and prosper. You thrive in a social and dynamic environment. It brings a good time that helps you upgrade your dreams and chase your goals.

17 Monday ~ Last Quarter Moon in Cancer 17.15

18 Tuesday

19 Wednesday

20 Thursday

21 Friday ~ Orionids Meteor Shower. October 2nd - November 7th

22 Saturday

23 Sunday

Zara is pleased to share that a window of opportunity opens, which offers a gateway to an enterprising time of working with your abilities. It kicks the stumbling blocks to the curb as you get involved with using your talents to draw prosperity into your world. It brings a busy time that offers growth and expansion. Developing an innovative venture brings improvement flowing into your life. It lets you connect with a circle of people who provide enterprising thoughts and engaging discussions. It sweeps away outworn areas and lets you walk a path that dazzles with golden opportunities.

24 Monday

25 Tuesday ~ New Moon in Scorpio 10:48
Partial Solar Eclipse

26 Wednesday

27 Thursday

28 Friday

29 Saturday

30 Sunday

Melody reveals that new people enter into your life to expand horizons. It brings a social aspect that highlights a path that draws abundance. Being open to new possibilities brings a pleasing outcome. It offers a fast-moving environment that is stable, progressive, and entertaining. It brings an element of surprise that draws excitement when news arrives that has you thinking about the potential in a new light. Information reaches you that amps up your life with new options. It brings inspiring adventures that team you up with kindred spirits. It lets you take advantage of a social phase where you can mingle with your tribe.

November

Sun	Mon	Tue	Wed	Thu	Fri	Sat
		1	2	3	4	5
6	7	8	9	10	11	12
13	14	15	16	17	18	19
20	21	22	23	24	25	26
27	28	29	30			

NOVEMBER ASTROLOGY

1ST - FIRST QUARTER MOON IN AQUARIUS 06.37

4TH - TAURIDS METEOR SHOWER. SEPTEMBER 7TH - DECEMBER 10TH

8TH - FULL MOON IN TAURUS 11:01 BEAVER MOON.

8TH - TOTAL LUNAR ECLIPSE

9TH - URANUS AT OPPOSITION

16TH - LAST QUARTER MOON IN LEO 13:27

17TH - LEONIDS METEOR SHOWER NOV 6TH-30TH

23RD - NEW MOON IN SAGITTARIUS 22:57

30TH - FIRST QUARTER MOON PISCES 14:36

New Moon

BEAVER MOON

31 Monday ~ Samhain/Halloween
All Hallows Eve

1 Tuesday ~ First Quarter Moon in Aquarius 06.37
All Saints' Day

2 Wednesday

3 Thursday

4 Friday ~ Taurids Meteor Shower. September 7th - December 10th

5 Saturday

6 Sunday

Fairy Summer is happy to share that you enjoy a rip-roaring time of social growth ahead. It lets you chart a course towards developing your circle of friends and embracing new opportunities to mingle. Focusing on expanding your social life brings a unique dynamic that offers exciting potential. It brings positive news that brightens your life. Confidence heightens as you get involved with an engaging chapter of lively discussions. It nurtures a stimulating environment that sparks creative possibilities. It brings a passion project that offers a path worth growing.

7 Monday

8 Tuesday ~ Full Moon in Taurus 11:01
Total Lunar Eclipse
Beaver Moon

9 Wednesday ~ Uranus at Opposition

10 Thursday

11 Friday ~ Remembrance Day (Canada)
Veterans Day

12 Saturday

13 Sunday

Fairy Adele confirms that a crossroads ahead brings a transition in your life. It is beneficial to listen to your inner guidance system during this transformation. Your intuition helps reveal new possibilities that draw stability, harmonizing foundations, and bringing a firm basis from which to grow your life. It offers an empowering time of exploring new options that spark creativity and magic. Honoring your gifts brings an influence that puts you in touch with your vision. Events transpire in your favor, and this good luck helps develop your goals. There is a chance to expand into a new area, bringing learning and growth into focus.

14 Monday

15 Tuesday

16 Wednesday ~ Last Quarter Moon in Leo 13:27

17 Thursday ~ Leonids Meteor Shower November 6-30

18 Friday

19 Saturday

20 Sunday

Pixie Trixie reveals that exciting news arrives that sees the path ahead shining with possibility. It brings a time of rapid change that sparks new goals. Nurturing life brings an enriching journey. It offers a chance to extend your reach into new areas and advance your vision forward. Lighter energy brings bright and cheerful times, which draws harmonizing foundations. Laying the groundwork for a unique journey forward brings an enriching chapter of advancing your situation. There is beautiful symmetry ahead as you move in alignment with a calling that speaks to your heart. Sweeping changes are on the horizon; a new adventure is looming.

21 Monday

22 Tuesday

23 Wednesday ~ New Moon in Sagittarius 22:57

24 Thursday ~ Thanksgiving Day (US)

25 Friday

26 Saturday

27 Sunday

Fairy Stella says to expect developments that center around self-development. Essential changes offer blessings that feed inspiration and fuel your desire to adapt and grow. You set off on a new adventure that sets an exciting tone for increasing your world. A richly creative process is at the crux of this enterprising time. It draws a gentle element that beautifully accents your current lifestyle. A bright and breezy environment offers a radiant aspect that illuminates new possibilities. It gives your life a reboot as it takes you towards a happy chapter ahead. Action and thought in motion bring creative energy that leads you to a branch of growth and prosperity.

December

Sun	Mon	Tue	Wed	Thu	Fri	Sat
				1	2	3
4	5	6	7	8	9	10
11	12	13	14	15	16	17
18	19	20	21	22	23	24
25	26	27	28	29	30	31

December Astrology

8th - Cold Moon. Moon Before Yule

8th - Full Moon in Gemini 04:07

8th - Mars at Opposition

13th - Geminids Meteor Shower. Dec 7th - 17th

16th - Last Quarter Moon in Virgo 08:56

21st - Ursids Meteor Shower December 17 - 25th

21st - Mercury at Greatest Eastern elongation.

21st - Yule/Winter Solstice at 09:48

23rd - New Moon in Capricorn 10:16

29th - Mercury Retrograde begins in Capricorn

30th - First Quarter Moon Aries 01:21

NEW MOON

COLD MOON

28 Monday

29 Tuesday

30 Wednesday ~ First Quarter Moon Pisces 14:36

1 Thursday

DECEMBER

2 Friday

3 Saturday

4 Sunday

Fairy Trixie says that new information ahead sprinkles fairy dust over your life. It brings a positive influence to light that sets the scene to nurture a more abundant landscape. Being open to new people and possibilities offers the chance to improve your social life and cultivate a sense of well-being in your world. Empowering energy is ready to flow into your world. Life reveals an active and dynamic time that becomes the key to progressing your goals forward. Improvement is swirling around your life; you can let the goodness in by being open to change. It does see an avenue opens that enables you to branch out and explore unchartered territory. It brings a social environment and lively conversations.

5 Monday

6 Tuesday

7 Wednesday

8 Thursday ~ Full Moon in Gemini 04:07
Cold Moon, Moon Before Yule
Mars at Opposition

9 Friday

10 Saturday

11 Sunday

Your fairy guides speak of favorable changes coming up that draw social engagement. It breaks old patterns and ways of thinking as it connects you with unique people and potential. It marks the beginning of an inspiring journey that offers new adventures with kindred spirits. It propels you toward an encouraging environment that provides room to grow your circle of friends. It brings lively discussions and the sharing of ideas. You may decide to switch gears and team up with others who can boost your world. Lively discussions bring a positive change. It does bring longer-term goals into focus. The energy of manifestation surrounds your life.

12 Monday

13 Tuesday ~ Geminids Meteor Shower. December 7-17

14 Wednesday

15 Thursday

16 Friday ~ Last Quarter Moon in Virgo 08:56

17 Saturday

18 Sunday ~ Hanukkah (begins at sunset)

Fairy Holly shares that good news arrives soon in a flurry of excitement. It lets you achieve real and lasting change as it brings a focus on growth and expansion. It brings options to go beyond your everyday routine and explore new heights of possibility. An exciting chapter blooms with a refreshing lightness. It places a strong emphasis on your social life and spending time with people who support your growth. It offers lively sessions of sharing thoughts and ideas with people who grow your life. It ripens conditions to nurture an interpersonal bond. Stimulating conversation brings an energizing time filled with light-hearted discussions.

19 Monday

20 Tuesday

21 Wednesday ~ Mercury at Greatest Eastern elongation of 20.1 degrees from Sun
Ursids Meteor Shower December 17 – 25
Yule/Winter Solstice at 09:48

22 Thursday

23 Friday ~ New Moon in Capricorn 10:16

24 Saturday

25 Sunday ~ Christmas Day

Pixie Ellie is excited to share that new options emerge in your life soon. It does let you touch down on a landscape that offers abundance and joy. Your sensitivity and emotional awareness guide this process. You crack the code to confidential matters when you reveal new possibilities around your love life. It brings the news that opens the door to a fresh start. It adds a buzz of romance and the dash of adventure that inspires growth. Moving out of your comfort zone lights up areas of kinship and companionship. It boosts your heart and blesses your world on many levels.

26 Monday ~ Boxing Day (Canada & UK)
Hanukkah (ends at sunset)
Christmas Day (observed)
Kwanzaa Begins

27 Tuesday

28 Wednesday

29 Thursday ~ Mercury Retrograde begins in Capricorn

30 Friday ~ First Quarter Moon Aries 01:21

31 Saturday ~ New Year's Eve

1 Sunday ~ New Year's Day
Kwanzaa ends

Fairy Danielle says that an outstanding opportunity arrives, and this brings a direction that aligns with your future vision. It lets you carve out quality time to spend developing a passion project. It brings a new enterprise that offers a creative aspect. It draws beneficial foundations that are grounded and happy. Life becomes sweeter, and this restores balance. It brings an opportunity to collaborate with an artistic character. You take an active role in advancing your situation. And your proactive approach is rewarded with new possibilities. Confidence is rising, and this is instrumental in dissolving barriers. It begins an expressive chapter that focuses on people and events that hold meaning to you.

About Crystal Sky

Crystal is passionate about the universe, helping others, and personal development. She writes yearly horoscopes diaries for each star sign. She produces a range of astrologically minded journals to celebrate the universal forces which affect us all. You can visit to learn more about Crystal's books and personal astrology readings by visiting the website.

www.psychic-emails.com

When not writing about the stars, you can find Crystal under them, gazing up at the abundance that surrounds us all, with her pup Henri by her side.

Made in the USA
Coppell, TX
03 December 2021

67073114R00111